In the
Shadows

In the
Shadows

I'm a Christian and I'm Depressed

Julie N. Hagaman

Acknowledgments

I want to give special thanks to all my family and friends who supported me when I went through depression. Special thanks to my aunt Trish who has been like a mother to me and is my biggest fan.

This book is dedicated to all Christians who are battling depression—You are not alone!

Disclaimer

The information in this book is not intended or implied to be a substitute for professional medical advice, diagnosis, or treatment. All content contained in this book is for general information purposes only. NEVER DISREGARD PROFESSIONAL MEDICAL ADVICE OR DELAY SEEKING MEDICAL TREATMENT BECAUSE OF SOMETHING YOU HAVE READ in this book. Please seek medical advice before beginning any treatment plan.

Are you having feelings of suicide or self-harm? Call the National Suicide Prevention Lifeline at 800-273-8255.

Prologue

Why did I write this book? More and more, I am hearing stories of Christian people, including pastors, who are attempting suicide. Many times there is no warning. Why is this? There seems to be a stigma around depression for Christians. There have been many times in my own life I wouldn't ask for help because I was afraid others would view me as a weak Christian. How could I be close to God and be depressed? This type of thinking is wrong and keeps many people from getting the help they desperately need.

As I am writing this book, I am going through one of the most challenging times of my life. Some days I feel like my entire world is crashing in. I have a relationship with God, but I am depressed. Yes, I said it. I am depressed. I am a Christian, and I am depressed.

You may be reading this book and be in the middle of depression yourself. First of all, you are not alone! You are not a bad Christian because you are depressed. You are not less of a person because you are depressed. Millions of people are going through the same thing you are right now. You owe it to yourself to get the help you need and not feel any guilt or shame about doing so.

Any ideas in this book are simply thoughts from my specific journey. They should not be taken as medical advice. Please don't be afraid to go to your doctor if you are experiencing extreme depression because there are many things they can do to support you during this time.

Julie Hagaman

There is therefore now no condemnation to them which are in Christ Jesus, who walk not after the flesh, but after the Spirit.

Romans 8:1

Chapter 1
Ditch the Shame

So you're a Christian, and you're depressed. Yes, I said it. You can be a Christian and be depressed. It is much more common than people are led to believe. Why is that? Many Christians think of depression as a weakness, and they don't want anyone to see their shortcomings. That is why we hear more and more stories about pastors and other church leaders taking their own lives. On the outside, they look fine, but on the inside, they are not ok.

Depression can hit anybody at any time. Pastors and pastor's wives get depressed. Missionaries get depressed. Praise and worship leaders get depressed. Depression doesn't cling to a specific category of people. It hits young and old, rich and poor, men and women--It affects everyone.

I grew up in the church. I was a pastor's daughter, and we were constantly at church. I remember hearing for years people talk about how depression came from Satan. While that may be true, they also pushed the stigma that if you were depressed, you were somehow not "right" with the Lord. After all, the Bible says the joy of the Lord is our strength, so how can we be depressed? The Bible says that God has not given us the spirit of fear, so how can we be anxious? People would cherry-pick verses to make it look like if you were depressed, you must be living in sin. Because of this stigma, many Christians today have trouble admitting they are depressed and often avoid getting the help they truly need.

What does the Bible have to say about depression? Believe it or not, quite a lot! God knew there would be times when we all faced depression, and he put examples for us in the Bible so that we would know we are not alone.

Let's talk about King David. What do you think about when you hear the words "King David"? I immediately think about how David killed Goliath. I think about how he was the apple of God's eye and specifically chosen by him to be one of the greatest leaders Israel has ever known. Is that the whole story? I'm afraid not. Sometimes we tend to skip over the messy stuff. You see, David made some mistakes. David had some family problems. David had some enemies that wanted to destroy him. Things were far from perfect for good ol' King David.

Can you imagine how David must have felt when his own children wanted to kill him? Can you imagine the shame he felt when he had a man murdered or the pain from losing his infant son? We don't have to imagine too hard because we can read

some of David's own words in the book of

Psalms. Let's look at those verses:

*O Lord, rebuke me not in thine anger, neither
chasten me in thy hot displeasure.*

*Have mercy upon me, O Lord; for I am weak: O Lord,
heal me; for my bones are vexed.*

*My soul is also sore vexed: but thou, O Lord, how
long?*

*Return, O Lord, deliver my soul: oh save me for thy
mercies' sake.*

*For in death there is no remembrance of thee: in the
grave who shall give thee thanks?*

*I am weary with my groaning; all the night make I my
bed to swim; I water my couch with my tears.*

*Mine eye is consumed because of grief; it waxeth old
because of all mine enemies.*

Psalms 6:1-7

That does not sound like the words of a happy

person! David paints a picture of a broken man,

crying out to God. He talks about how he cried all

night until his bed was wet with tears. Have you ever been there? David was.

Not only was David depressed, but he also wasn't afraid to tell people about it! He would go around singing songs to people just like this one. Can you imagine what would happen if we went around singing, "I'm so depressed! I cried myself to sleep. I need help!" We would be much too worried about what people would think of us to try and do what David did—but maybe David was on the right track.

David understood the importance of getting our feelings out in the open. He understood the importance of expressing our grief and sadness and not holding those feelings in. We, as Christians, need to take a lesson from King David. It is okay to let people know how you are feeling. It is okay to let people know when you need help. Believe it or not, there isn't a person in this world who has not experienced depression at some point in their life. You are not alone.

YOU DON'T HAVE TO FEEL SHAME ABOUT FEELING DEPRESSED! If you take nothing else from this book, please understand this—stop the feelings of guilt. Guilt makes depression worse than it already is! You don't need to feel guilty about your feelings. If you have stolen a car, you have something to feel guilty about, but feeling guilty about being depressed doesn't make sense.

Much of the stigma surrounding depression has been hyped up in our imagination. I remember going to a mentor of mine and sharing that I was going through a major depression. I was sure they would talk to me about how I needed to get right with God or blame the depression on something I was doing wrong. What happened was quite the opposite! Instead, they began to share how they had gone through the same thing! We laughed and cried

together, and I left feeling like I was no longer

alone. Remember, EVERYONE has been affected

by depression at some point.

Let's look at another example in the Bible—

Job. If anyone had a reason to be depressed, it

would be him! He lost nearly everything he had—

including his children! He ripped apart the robe he

was wearing when he heard the bad news. Why did

he do this? It was an outward sign of the grief and

despair he was feeling on the inside.

The worst part of this story was when Job's

friends came on the scene. Instead of trying to

comfort Job, they attempted to show him what he

was doing wrong. They wanted to show him all the

reasons they thought he deserved this terrible

ordeal. Have you ever had friends like that? I know I

have! You are depressed and in despair, and

instead of comforting you, your friends only try to tell

you what you are doing wrong. These kinds of

people have been around since the beginning.

Everyone in Job's group thought they were doing

him a favor by showing him the error of his

ways. Many people in your life mean well, but they

don't realize how much harm they are doing. Instead

of helping you, they are just creating more guilt and

shame and adding to your despair! If you have

someone in your life that is going through intense

depression, don't lecture them. Just listen and love.

God himself rebuked Job's friends! It wasn't Job's

fault he was going through this mess, and God had

his back right in the middle of it. God let Job's

friends know they had done the wrong thing in

blaming him for the troubles he was

facing. Sometimes you go through times of deep

despair and hardship, but you must hold on to the

fact that God has your back through it all. Even when your friends hurt you, God is waiting for you with open arms. He will listen to you when you cry out to Him and send you comfort in your time of sorrow.

God restored Job. He didn't tell Job, "Well, you're depressed, and in despair, so you are a sinner!" That's not how God works. God started by showing Job His greatness. He showed him just how mighty He is! There is nothing God cannot do, and He wanted to make sure Job knew that. Amid great despair, it is easy to start thinking our situation can never change. God, however, would disagree. He wants us to know there is nothing too hard for Him to fix. There is hope! Let me reiterate—There is hope for you!

You may be facing the biggest battle of your life. You may feel like your life is over. I want to encourage you that you are not alone. Christians all

over the world feel the same way! Don't give up yet,

because God has your back just like He had

Jobs. When we are going through tough times, it is

easy to forget that God is still there, but God loves

you, and you are not alone! You matter. You are

loved.

Why should you not feel shame over being depressed?

____

____

____

____

____

What can you learn about depression from the story of Job?

____

____

____

____

____

What is one thing from this chapter you can apply to your life right now?

____

____

____

____

____

Notes

Finally, brethren, whatsoever things are true, whatsoever things are honest, whatsoever things are just, whatsoever things are pure, whatsoever things are lovely, whatsoever things are of good report; if there be any virtue, and if there be any praise, think on these things.

Philippians 4:8

Chapter 2
What do you think?

One of the most challenging battles we face when dealing with depression is in our minds. Our minds can spin us into a place of complete and utter panic in no time flat! The things we think about can shape everything we do during the day. It also shapes the way we feel.

I fight this battle all the time. I will be driving down the road, and suddenly a thought will come into my head about something that *might* happen. Before I know it, I have imagined an entire scenario of bad things happening in perfect detail. Then begins the spiral—the panic. I find myself thinking the world is about to cave in around me, and it all starts with a single thought!

What can we do when we get into those situations? One of the ways I deal with this problem is to remind myself of this—I may be feeling like the world is caving in on me right now, but I only think this way because my emotions have taken over. I won't always feel this way. In times of despair, we can easily forget that we will not always be sad. In a moment of panic, it is hard to get our heads wrapped around this idea, but we must! The worst thing you can do is make major decisions during one of these attacks.

I can give you an example from my own life. I am a teacher, and one year I was able to get my children enrolled in the school where I was teaching. One day, during a period of extreme panic, I withdrew my children from school. At that moment, I thought I couldn't handle teaching and having my kids at school too. Terrible, disastrous scenarios began to play over and over again in my mind. I decided in a moment of panic to pull my children out of the school. Later, I regretted it. At the time, it felt like my world was caving in, and I had to do something about it. In all actuality, things were not as bad as they seemed, but at that moment, I wasn't thinking clearly.

In a moment of extreme panic or despair, your brain goes into a state of fight or flight. You immediately want to do something to change your situation. You must resist that urge! You may feel like quitting your job—wait! You may feel like hurting yourself—wait! If you can get yourself to pause for a moment—to just wait for a little while—you can often stop bad decisions from being made in a moment of panic.

So what can we do? First of all, you need to recognize when your mind starts to wonder. It is easy to get caught up inside your thoughts and let yourself spiral out of control. When that first thought enters your mind, do something to shift your thoughts. Start singing at the top of your lungs! Call up a friend or loved one and ask them about their day. Turn on a comedy show and laugh a little. Read a scripture passage. Listen to anointed music. Listen to an uplifting message from an evangelist or teacher. Do something to keep your mind from stewing on all those negative thoughts.

Secondly, when the thoughts start to come, ask yourself, is this something that is definitely going to happen or something that *might* happen. 95% of the things you worry about never actually happen. Let that get into your head. 95% of the scenarios you think up never happen! Instead of imagining the worst possible scenario, stop and imagine the best possible scenario. Let it play out in your mind from start to finish. Imagine everything going right. Will that change your situation? No, but it can stop you from spiraling into a panic attack and give you a new perspective. After all, if I am going to waste my energy thinking about things that will probably never

happen, at least they can be good things!

My dad always used to tell me, "Garbage in-

garbage out." What does that mean? If you are

constantly filling yourself up with negativity, that's

what will come out of you. I found this out the hard

way in my life. I have always commuted to work, and

at one point, I was driving about 80 miles to work

every day. During that time, I would listen to the

news on the radio. It seemed like I was always

depressed! One day, someone told me to stop

listening to the news as I drove to work. Instead, I

replaced the news with audio bible scriptures,

different podcasts, or uplifting music. I could not

believe the difference it made in my everyday

life! Before, I was filling up every day with

negativity. Every morning I would hear about people

who were in car crashes, national disasters, riots,

and other accidents. Then I would go on to work and wonder why I was feeling down. I was doing it to myself and didn't even know it!

What does the Bible have to say about our thoughts? Philippians 4:8 tells us to think about good things. Paul reminds us to set our thoughts on things that will uplift us, not tear us down. You see, even Paul knew that it is easy for the mind to get pulled to the dark side. We have to set our minds on thinking about good things—it doesn't come naturally.

In 2 Corinthians 10:5, Paul talks about how we have to take every thought captive. It is almost like we are in a war with our minds. It is so easy to fall into a downward spiral. We have to train like soldiers to take those negative thoughts captive. It won't come easy at first, but the more you practice stopping those negative thoughts at their root, the easier it will become.

Our mind is a battlefield. It would like to destroy you if it could. The good news is you are not alone! You have the Holy Spirit to help you in your daily battle. The Bible calls the Holy Spirit our comforter. He can speak peace to your mind in the middle of the biggest storm. He can be that rope you are holding onto when everything else is swaying in the wind. Don't be afraid to call out to God during those times when you feel yourself spiraling out of control. It is the last thing our flesh wants us to do, but it is often the most helpful. When we are in this kind of situation, it is not easy to stop and seek God. Sometimes all you can do is cry out the name of Jesus! Let me tell you—He hears your cry! Psalms 34:15 says, "The eyes of the LORD *are* upon the righteous, and his ears are open unto their cry." God hears you when you cry out to Him!

So let's review what we have learned so far about our thoughts. Our thoughts can cause us to spiral out of control, but we can stop the decline before it is too late. First, recognize what is happening. We need to be aware when our minds are about to play "what if" situations. Realize that 95% of those scenarios never happen. Replace the bad scenario with a best-case scenario. Make yourself turn your thoughts to good things by listening to worship music or positive sermons, by reading scriptures, by talking to a friend, and by calling upon the Lord. Try some of these ideas and see if it helps stop your mind from heading towards that downward spiral.

Finally, realize that sometimes we get in a situation where it seems we can't control our thoughts at all. If you are at that point, I urge you to talk to your doctor and get medical support. Chemical changes in the brain can cause thought patterns that these simple strategies can't help. Don't be afraid to ask

for help! You are worth it!

What do you spend the most time thinking about each day?

____

____

____

____

____

What is one thing you can do when your thoughts start to spiral out of control?

____

____

____

____

____

What is one thing from this chapter you can apply to your life right now?

____

____

____

____

____

____

____

Notes

But he was wounded for our transgressions, he was bruised for our iniquities: the chastisement of our peace was upon him; and with his stripes we are healed.

Isaiah 53:5

Chapter 3
Check your temperature

Many times we are quick to blame the devil for everything bad that happens. Sometimes, however, there are other underlying causes. Many health problems can cause depression. This chapter will look at some of the common medical causes of depression and what you can do to find help.

One of the most significant battles I faced was with PMS. Many women can relate with me in this! The problem was, I didn't understand why my PMS seemed so extreme. I had no idea there was any such thing as Premenstrual Dysphoric Disorder (PMDD). I had no idea that my hormones were causing me to lose my mind every month. On the worst days, I felt like my life was falling apart. Nothing was different from the day before, but my body and my hormones were telling me there was. I felt out of control. I felt like I wasn't going to make it. This was happening every month!

I want you to understand that this type of extreme PMS is not typical! You should not feel out of control any day of the month! If you feel this way, it is not because your thoughts aren't right or you are doing something wrong—it is all about your hormones. Many people suggest exercise, natural remedies, and diet changes for extreme PMS, but I urge you to visit your physician. There is help out there—you just need to ask for it. If you go to a doctor who is not sympathetic to what you are going through, find a new one! The most important thing is to get help! Don't try to go it alone.

Another trigger for depression can be medications. Have you started feeling down lately and have no clue why? Check the side effects of some of the medicines you are taking. You will find that depression is a known side effect of many common medications. If you need the medication, you may feel trapped. Often, there are alternative medications your doctor can prescribe that do not affect you in the same way. The important thing is to talk with your doctor and let them know you feel this way and are concerned about your medication. They can take it from there.

Another cause of depression can be substance abuse. It may be alcohol, drugs, or even pain medication that is causing your depression. What happens when you take a drug? You initially get a high. You feel better. Then suddenly, you drop down and are worse off than you were before. Every time you cycle through those highs and lows, your depression gets worse and worse. I implore you to see a doctor or a professional counselor and get the help you need. Once you conquer your problems with substance abuse, your depression problems will probably go with it.

Did you know depression can be genetic? You can be more prone to be depressed if there is a history of it in your family. You can do nothing to change who you are, but you can help your current situation. Seek the help of professionals—your doctor, pastor, or counselor. Don't wait until your life is out of control, but be proactive in getting the help you need. If you know it runs in your family, have your loved ones keep an eye out for you. Don't walk the path alone.

Some people battle with Seasonal Affective Disorder (SAD). Many times this type of depression occurs during the fall and winter months. Have you ever found yourself feeling down during the winter months? You may have a form of SAD. Light therapy can be beneficial for this type of depression. Because of the change of season, we aren't getting enough sunlight, and light therapy can counteract that. Vitamin D supplements are also helpful.

Chronic illness can be a major cause of depression. Imagine being in pain every day of your life. Who wouldn't be depressed? All over the world, people are facing illnesses that cause debilitating pain. Maybe the illness you are facing doesn't have a cure, and you feel like there is no hope.

My mother battled cancer at a young age. She was in significant pain, and the medicine they were giving her wasn't helping much. I remember one day she said, "I understand why people in extreme pain consider taking their own life. I wouldn't do it, but I understand now." When you are in a place where all you know is pain every day, life can seem hopeless.

There are two things I need you to know. First of

all, call out to God. He is still a healer. His word tells

us that by the stripes on His back, we were made

whole. Secondly, find a good physician who will give

you proper pain management and deal with your

depression. There is hope. Don't give up the fight.

Did you know the food we eat can also influence

how we feel each day? When we stuff our bodies full

of junk, that is how we feel--junky! When we stuff

ourselves with junk food, our bodies don't run

right. We feel sick and sluggish, and that can make

depression much worse. Do a web search on the

link between nutrition and depression. I was amazed

at how many medical studies have been done on this

topic. One study even showed a direct link between

the amount of fast food we take in and

depression! Talk to your doctor about a healthy

eating plan that will help improve your life—body, mind, and soul.

What about medication for depression? That is a question I get asked a lot. If you have gotten to a point in your life where your depression is causing harm to you or your family, you need to talk to your doctor about it. Don't wait around for it to get better. Get help! God gave man the wisdom to create medicines that can help you when the chemicals in your brain just aren't working the way they should. Do not feel shame or guilt about needing medical help.

I have been to that point in my personal life. I was at a place where I could no longer help myself. I remember sitting in the doctor's office crying because of how bad I felt. I also remember how much the medicine "evened" me out. I wasn't having those low crashes anymore. I was able to function without falling apart. I was able to keep going.

Taking medicine was not without problems. I had to try a few different kinds before I found something that worked for me. The first medicine I was on took away the lows I was experiencing, but it also took away the highs in life. I wasn't sad, but I wasn't overly happy either. I missed those times of great joy. I talked to my doctor, and we tried some other medications that controlled my depression without depriving me of my happiness. Don't be afraid to speak with your doctor if the medicines don't work the first time. It is a process, but it is worth the time to get it right.

There are so many physical factors that can cause depression. Some of these we have no control over. Changes to our diet or medications can manage other factors. Whatever the cause of your depression—don't ignore it. Get the help and

support you need and deserve.

44

What are some physical causes of depression?

____

____

____

____

____

____

What are two practical tips from this chapter that help combat depression?

____

____

____

____

____

____

What is one thing from this chapter you can apply to your life right now?

____

____

____

____

____

____

____

Notes

Chapter 4
Give up the control!

Every one of us goes through bad times in life—no one is exempt. Maybe you have lost a loved one. Perhaps you are going through sickness. Maybe you have been betrayed by a spouse or a good friend. You may have lost your job and are struggling financially. These kinds of events can knock the wind right out of you.

Often, after a traumatic event, we go through a period of depression. This is perfectly normal. It would not be normal to remain happy when you just lost your best friend or your child is diagnosed with a disease. You are not doing something wrong when you are sad. Remember King David and his song? Everyone goes through times when they cry themselves to sleep because of their circumstances in life.

If, however, during this time of mourning, you cannot get out of bed or have feelings about hurting yourself, you need to seek help right away. Sadness is normal, but extreme feelings brought on by a crisis must be addressed right away! Go to your doctor. Visit your pastor. Talk with your counselor. The most important thing is—**get help** somewhere.

Some situations in your life are temporary and won't last forever. Others may stay for the rest of your life. You must begin to understand that there are some situations you have no control over. You can't change them.

When I was young, remote controls for T.V's were just becoming popular. My sister and I would fight over who would get the remote control. She usually won because she was older and bigger than me! Often in our life, we fight to gain control over our circumstances. We struggle every day to try and "fix" things that sometimes just cannot be fixed.

Trying to fix things outside of my control was a huge one for me. I would get in a complete uproar over situations I had no control over. One of the most significant battles for me was with my family. I tried my best to "fix" my husband and children when they had a problem. Instead, I was only creating more problems for myself. You cannot control what others do. Let me say that again. You cannot control what others do! You can't make them do the right thing or go the right path. We can pray, but the rest is up to them.

I had a huge turning point in my own life when I finally came to terms with the idea that I could not control what others do. It seems so simple, but I wasted a lot of years anguishing over other people's actions. Let me give you a hypothetical example.

Sylvia has been married for 12 years. Her husband used to go to church with her every week but now refuses to go. Suddenly, he wants to hang out with his friends all the time and spends no time at home. Sylvia is distraught and is constantly trying to think of ways to fix his situation. She plans romantic weekends together, but he cancels them. She sends him loving text messages, but he doesn't respond. She plays Christian tv shows in the house during the day, but he just changes the channel. Sylvia tries every plan she can think of, but things get worse and worse. Suddenly, Sylvia finds herself in deep depression because she is not able to change her husband.

Does this sound familiar? Maybe it's not a husband, but a family member or close friend. Either way, we can get so caught up in trying to make

things right we run ourselves into the ground. What
can we do?

First, we have to figure out that we cannot change
someone else. Once you truly do that, it will be like a
weight is lifted off of your shoulders. I will give my
children all the love and support they need, but in the
end, they are responsible for their actions. I will give
my husband all the love and support he needs, but
he is accountable for the choices he makes. Once
you give up the idea that you have to control the
situation, it can bring so much more peace to your
life.

So what can we do if we see a loved one making
bad choices or decisions? Paul tells us that in
everything, we should let our petitions be made
known to God. (Philippians 4:6) When you don't
know what to do, take it to the Lord. Sometimes we
have to say, "God, I can't do anything about this

situation, but I know you can." Once you give it to God, you have to let it go. When the thoughts come again, bringing worry and despair to your mind, bring them to God. Bring it to God again and again—as many times as it takes. This, however, is the critical part—give it to God and don't pick it back up again. I know that is easier said than done, but we spend way too much of our time tormenting ourselves over things we have zero control over. Let go!

There are many things in life that we have no control over. When we try to fix those situations on our own, we can cause ourselves to spiral out of control. It is only when we give up control that we can truly find peace.

What are some things you have no control over in
your life?

____

____

____

____

____

____

Why does it make no sense to dwell on
circumstances we cannot control?

____

____

____

____

____

____

What is one thing from this chapter you can apply to
your life right now?

____

____

____

____

____

____

____

Notes

And it came to pass, when the evil spirit from God was upon Saul, that David took an harp, and played with his hand: so Saul was refreshed, and was well, and the evil spirit departed from him.

1 Samuel 16:23

Chapter 5
Singing in the Rain

There is a story in the Bible about a King named Saul. This story gives us a true example of just how powerful music can be.

And it came to pass, when the evil spirit from God was upon Saul, that David took an harp, and played with his hand: so Saul was refreshed, and was well, and the evil spirit departed from him.

1 Samuel 16:23

Whenever Saul would become angry and depressed, they would bring in a harp player, and as he played music, the spirit of depression would leave.

Scientific research has found that music has therapeutic properties beyond our understanding. Do a web search on the effects of music on depression, and you will see dozens of scientific studies proving the link between music and depression relief. Music is therapeutic and can be a great asset to your depression tool kit.

I watched a video one time about a man with dementia. At the beginning of the video, he wasn't able to answer simple questions. Then, they began to play music for him—the kind of music from his youth. Suddenly, you could see the light come back into his eyes! After listening to the music, he was able to talk with the interviewer coherently for about 20 minutes. What does this have to do with depression? We need to realize that music dramatically affects the brain and can even change the way our brains make connections!

What kind of music should I listen to? That is a great question! My first recommendation is to listen to anointed Gospel music. There is something about playing the music of someone filled with the Spirit that seems to chase the evil spirits away. We can see this in the case of King Saul. When David, who was full of the Spirit of God, played his harp, the spirit of depression had to go! If you face a depression

with roots in the spiritual (see chapter 12), this is an

excellent technique to use. The enemy can't stay in

the presence of the Holy Spirit, so playing anointed

music can make demons flee.

Uplifting music with positive messages can help

boost your spirit. Read the lyrics of the songs you

are listening to. Are they positive or negative? Do

they just point out all the bad things happening in

your life, or are they focusing your mind on good

things?

Many people find listening to classical music has

a positive effect on their depression. There are no

words, but the music itself is uplifting and

encouraging and can positively impact your life.

I made a playlist of songs that made me feel good

and put them on my phone. These were songs that

reminded me of the good things happening in my

life. Listening to this playlist in the morning helped me start my day more encouraged and ready to go.

Ultimately, you need to find out what music works for you. What do you like? What music lifts your spirit? Make a decision today to incorporate more music into your daily life and see if it affects your depression symptoms.

Why is it so essential to incorporate music into your everyday life?

____

____

____

____

____

What songs instantly "perk you up" when you play them?

____

____

____

____

____

What is one thing from this chapter you can apply to your life right now?

____

____

____

____

____

____

Notes

*I will ask the Father, and he will give you another
helper who will be with you forever.*

John 14:16

Chapter 6
I Want to Be Alone!

When I am depressed, I tend to isolate myself from the people I love. I find myself spending more and more time alone and consumed with my thoughts. Why is that a problem? Often, spending too much time alone can cause you to spiral out of control. Even though it is hard and often uncomfortable, we need to make an effort to spend time with other people and less time alone.

What's wrong with being alone? We all need alone time at some point, but when you are going through a depression, isolating yourself can lead to a dramatic increase in despair and feelings of sadness.

Many scientific studies talk about the correlation between depression and being alone. You may feel like staying isolated, but it is the worst thing you can

do.

What can we do to be more social? The first thing

I suggest is to surround yourself with friends and

family who can support you at this time in your

life. This is not just anybody. Some people will do

nothing but tear you down. You need people around

you who will encourage you and build you up. You

need people who are willing to be there at any time

of day. You need people willing to sit and just listen

and not judge you for what you are going through. If

you have such a person in your life, I encourage you

to reach out to them and share what you are going

through. They can be the lifeline for you in a time

when you seem to be drowning in despair.

Not everyone has a friend that they can turn to for

support. What do you do then? There are various

options available if you do not feel comfortable talking to a friend or family member.

First of all, consider talking to a counselor. This may be scary if you have never done it before. You may feel apprehensive about sharing your feelings with a complete stranger, but sometimes that is exactly what you need to do. A counselor is specially trained in dealing with depression and can support you in ways that a friend or family member cannot. I remember the first time I talked with a professional about my depression. I cried and talked with them for an hour. When I left, I felt like someone understood what I was going through. I knew I was not alone. A good counselor can be an excellent support system for you when you are going through a hard time.

Secondly, join a local church. This is huge! Find a church that has opportunities for fellowship with the members. Find a church where the people are friendly and want to establish relationships with you. The Bible says in Hebrews 10:25, "Not forsaking the assembling of ourselves together, as the manner of some is; but exhorting one another: and so much the more, as ye see the day approaching."

What does it mean to exhort? Exhort means to encourage. You need to be a part of a church where the members encourage one another! We are there to build one another up, not tear each other down. That is the job of the church! It should be a place where you can go to find encouragement in the Lord and peace in your heart.

Another great way to spend time with other people is through support groups. They have support groups for various subjects—singles groups, weight loss groups, parent groups, and much more! Don't be afraid to join a support group in your local area. It is so freeing to be with a group of people who are going through the same things you are. It helps you realize you are not alone.

Another way you can put yourself in more social situations is by taking classes. This is not only a great way to meet like-minded people, but it is also an excellent way to enhance your knowledge and skills. Is there something you enjoy doing? Why not take a class and hone up your skills? Is there something you would like to learn or try out for the first time? Try signing up for a beginner class and see if it is for you.

Another great way to get yourself out there is by volunteering. Many non-profit organizations are in desperate need of help. Not only will volunteering help you mentally, but it will also help others. It is a win-win situation!

When you are going through depression, the last thing you want to do is be with other people, but that is the exact thing you need to do! Being alone when you are depressed can cause your thoughts to spiral out of control. Forcing yourself to step out of your comfort zone and get out there and be social is exactly what you need to do. Yes, it is uncomfortable. Yes, it is hard. Yes, it is exactly what you need to do. So make a plan right now to get out there and spend time with others. Whatever you have to do—do it!

Why is it so important to spend time with others?

____

____

____

____

____

What are two ways you can spend more time with others?

____

____

____

____

____

What is one thing from this chapter you can apply to your life right now?

____

____

____

____

____

____

Notes

For I know the thoughts that I think toward you, saith the LORD, thoughts of peace, and not of evil, to give you an expected end

Jeremiah 29:11

Chapter 7
Find your passion

Many years ago, I worked as an assistant manager for a large department store chain. I went to school to be a teacher, but teaching jobs were few and far between, so I decided to try something different. This job paid very well, so I was excited to start.

Now, one thing you need to know about me is that I like to do everything well. In school, I wanted all A's. In my job, I wanted to be the best. Imagine my frustration when I realized I was a terrible assistant manager. I was not good at managing employees. I always wanted to say positive, uplifting things to my employees and did not want to deal with drama. If you have ever worked in retail, you know this is not a good combination!

Pretty soon, I was miserable. I did not enjoy what I was doing, and I wasn't good at it at all. Talk about being depressed! I felt as low as I could go.

I finally got up the nerve to leave that job and follow my passion. When I began my teaching career, it was like I was made for that job. I worked with children with special needs, and I felt happier and more fulfilled than ever before.

When you get up every day and work at a job you hate, you will often go through each day sad and depressed. If you get up each day and are working in the position God designed you for, you will find yourself in a place of peace and contentment.

How do we find that place God designed for us? First of all, you need to find your passion. What are you passionate about? What do you enjoy most? What are you naturally good at doing? When I asked those questions, a picture may have automatically popped into your mind. Maybe you saw yourself

leading corporate meetings, cutting hair, or teaching

children. Perhaps you are not sure what your passion

is. That is okay too! Keep looking for it. When you

find it, you will know it is exactly where you are

meant to be.

Do you know God specifically designed us for a

purpose? He created us with a specific purpose in

mind. Isn't that amazing?   God made me exactly

how he wanted so I could fulfill my destiny. If I am

doing something I was not created to do, that can

cause friction and misery.

Let me give you an example. Think about a

hammer. A hammer is a tool that is made for a

specific purpose—to pound in nails. If I tried to use

that hammer as a screwdriver, I would get frustrated

pretty quickly because that is not what a hammer is

made for.

In the same way, we are like tools designed by God for a specific purpose. When we are doing what we were created to do, everything runs seamlessly. However, when we try to do tasks we were not designed for, we face friction, which can bring on depression.

You don't understand, Julie! I hate my job, but I can't just leave it. I have to support my family! I would never tell a person to leave a job that would put their family in financial distress. At the same time, have you opened yourself up to the possibility that God has more for your life?

I once had a good friend who hated his job. He had to support his family, so he couldn't just leave it but would often complain about how much he hated the position. I would often come across jobs that I thought he would love—and that would pay the same amount! He never put in another application because he was convinced he would never get a position he liked. He never even gave it a chance!

I believe God wants us to be doing what we were designed for! I prayed for the right job for a long time, but I also submitted dozens of applications and resumes while I prayed. God opened up the door that was right for me. When I started doing what I loved, my entire life changed! If I would have given up and been satisfied working at a job I didn't enjoy, I would have never known how it felt to fulfill my destiny. Are you trying to move towards your passion, or have you given up? If you are not working a job you are passionate about, why not put in one application a week for a job you would love. If you don't get the position, you are only out a few minutes a week, but it could change your life forever if you do get the job. Dare to dream like never before!

Maybe it is impossible to change your career, but that does not mean you cannot follow your passion! There are other ways to do what you were created to do! Use your passion to help those around you! Do you love to paint? Paint pictures for your friends or donate them to fundraisers. Do you love children? Offer to babysit for free one night for a mom who may be burned out and frustrated. Do you love working outside? Why not help take care of the yard of an older person in your church or neighborhood? There are many ways you can use what you are passionate about to help others.

God created you with a specific purpose in mind. He made you, like that hammer, to do a particular job on this earth. When you are doing what God created you to do, you can find true happiness and fulfillment. When you are doing something you were not designed for, you may find yourself sinking into

depression and despair.

What are some things you are passionate about?

____

____

____

____

____

____

What are two ways you can start using your passion each week?

____

____

____

____

____

____

What is one thing from this chapter you can apply to your life right now?

____

____

____

____

____

____

____

Notes

He that walketh with wise men shall be wise: but a companion of fools shall be destroyed.

Proverbs 13:20

Chapter 8
Unclog Your Drain!

Have you ever had a clogged drain? Something

blocks the water from getting through, and it causes

your sink or toilet to back up. It can make a real

mess! Until you clear the blockage, the water will not

flow, and the mess will continue. Our lives work the

same way!

Toxic people can clog your mental drain! What is

a toxic person? A toxic person is anyone who makes

you feel worse than you already do. Have you ever

went to visit someone and left feeling terrible? That

is a toxic person. Let's look at some of the traits of a

toxic person.

First of all, they are always complaining. They will

complain about the neighbors. They will complain

about their coworkers. They will complain about their

family members. Once you leave, they will complain

about you! These types of people always look for the

bad in everything. If they can't find something to complain about, they will make something up.

Secondly, the toxic person is never satisfied. If you give them a Wal-Mart gift card for their birthday, they wanted a Target gift card. If you bring them roses, they wanted carnations. If you visit once a week, they are angry you don't see them twice a week. If you give them $50, they needed $100. They are never satisfied with anything you do.

To the toxic person, you will never be good enough. If you tell them you got a new job, they will tell you about someone who got a better job. If you got an award, they would let you know that trophies don't mean anything. If you get dressed up and feel good about yourself, they will find something wrong with your hair or outfit. To the toxic person, you will never be good enough.

The toxic person likes to manipulate. They will use put-downs and complaints to try and get you to do what they want you to do. They will try to control you by "gaslighting" you. What is gaslighting? It is a type of manipulation that gets you to question your reality, memories, or perceptions. Examples of gaslighting could be:

- Stop acting crazy.

- You're just paranoid.

- I was just joking! Stop being so sensitive!

- You just like to stir up trouble.

- That never happened!

- It's no big deal.

Have you heard some of these comments before? Chances are, you were being manipulated, and you didn't know it.

The toxic person loves to crush your dreams. They will love to point out the many reasons why your dreams will never become a reality. They will do whatever they can to make sure you never rise above the level they are at right now.

As I have been describing the traits of a toxic person, maybe the image of someone has jumped into your mind. If you are going through depression, a toxic person can make it ten times worse. So what can you do?

If at all possible, remove yourself from the life of a toxic person. This person is not worth your life, and if they are sucking all the joy out of you, you need to get away from them. Your life is worth more. Yes, it may cause some drama if you have to let go of a friend or a family member, but in the end, it will only make you better.

Sometimes, you cannot remove yourself from a toxic person. If that is the case, I recommend giving yourself as much distance from this person as you possibly can. Also, make sure you spend a lot of time with positive people who will uplift you to counteract the damage a toxic person can cause. If you have to spend time with a toxic person, keep reminding yourself, "This person is toxic. I will not allow myself to be pulled down to their level. I will not allow myself to be affected by their drama."

Sometimes, you may not realize just how much people can affect your mood. Ask yourself the question, do I feel better or worse after I spend time with them? If you feel worse, it may be you are dealing with a toxic person.

A toxic person in your life can increase depression in dramatic ways. They can increase feelings of negativity and sadness. If at all possible, set yourself apart from these people. If not possible, then distance yourself the best you can. Surround yourself with people who will lift you up and support you!

Who are some toxic people in your life?

____

____

____

____

____

____

What are two ways you can distance or separate yourself from that toxic person?

____

____

____

____

____

What is one thing from this chapter you can apply to your life right now?

____

____

____

____

____

____

____

Notes

*Death and life are in the power of the tongue: and they
that love it shall eat the fruit thereof.*

Proverbs 18:21

Chapter 9
You Can!

What do you talk about every day? Do you find yourself talking about everything going wrong in your life, or are you talking about what is going right? In this chapter, we are going to discuss how what you say affects how you feel.

The Bible has a lot to say about what we should speak. Let's look at a few of those verses.

Death and life are in the power of the tongue: and they that love it shall eat the fruit thereof.

Proverbs 18:21

A wholesome tongue is a tree of life: but perverseness therein is a breach in the spirit.

Proverbs 15:4

The mouth of the just bringeth forth wisdom: but the froward tongue shall be cut out.

Proverbs 10:31

The Bible has so much to say about how we speak because it is so vitally important! We learned in the previous chapter how toxic people could make your depression worse In the same way, you can make your depression worse by the things you say.

Do you listen to yourself each day? Are you tearing yourself down or trying to build yourself up. Are you constantly saying things like:

- I hate my body.

- I'm so fat.

- I will never be successful.

- I'm always two steps behind.

- I can never get ahead.

- I never get a break.

When you are saying these things, you are telling your brain that this is reality! You have to train yourself to speak differently if you are ever going to think differently.

There have been dozens of scientific studies proving that using verbal self-affirmations can change how you feel about yourself. If you are constantly putting yourself down, that is what your brain will come to believe. If you are continually speaking good things about yourself, then your brain will adapt to this new information and change your way of thinking. I know it sounds simple, but in essence, you are what you speak.

What kind of positive affirmations should you speak each day? First of all, I would start with positive scriptures. Here are a few I have used in the past.

I can do all things through Christ which strengtheneth me.

Philippians 4:13

No weapon that is formed against thee shall prosper; and every tongue that shall rise against thee in judgment thou shalt condemn. This is the heritage of the servants of the Lord, and their righteousness is of me, saith the Lord.

Isaiah 54:17

Ye are of God, little children, and have overcome them: because greater is he that is in you, than he that is in the world.

1 John 4:4

When the enemy shall come in like a flood, the Spirit of the Lord shall lift up a standard against him.

Isaiah 59:19b

The Lord is my light and my salvation; whom shall I fear? the Lord is the strength of my life; of whom shall I be afraid?

Psalms 27:1

What shall we then say to these things? If God be for us, who can be against us?

Romans 8:31

I will praise thee; for I am fearfully and wonderfully made: marvellous are thy works; and that my soul knoweth right well.

Psalms 139:14

Have not I commanded thee? Be strong and of good courage; be not afraid, neither be thou dismayed: for the LORD thy God is with thee whithersoever thou goest.

Joshua 1:9

These are just a few of the amazing scriptures that you can speak every day. Speaking these scriptures each day will both uplift you and encourage you.

Would you believe positive affirmations can help protect your self-esteem? Research has proven that people who speak positive affirmations each day have fewer negative thoughts about themselves. That is amazing! The first time I made a list of affirmations and started reading them out loud, I felt a little bit silly, but I was at the point where I would try anything if I thought there was a chance it might work.

No one can tell you what you need on your list. You make your list of affirmations and tailor them to your life. Here are a few of the affirmations I use myself.

- I am blessed and highly favored.

- Good things are coming my way today.

- I am skilled at what I do.

- I am creative and talented, and I am always coming up with new ideas.

- I am an asset to my team at work and help others each day.

- Others value me, and I value myself.

Choose some positive affirmations and make your own list. What you say makes a difference in how you feel!

Why is it important to watch what we say?

____

____

____

____

____

What are two positive affirmations you can say each day?

____

____

____

____

____

What is one thing from this chapter you can apply to your life right now?

____

____

____

____

____

____

Notes

In everything give thanks: for this is the will of God in Christ Jesus concerning you.

1 Thessalonians 5:18

Chapter 10
An Attitude of Gratitude

Sometimes, when we are going through depression, all we can see are the bad things in our lives. All of our focus is on what is going wrong and why we should be miserable. The more we look at our problems, the more we can spiral out of control.

Our minds are tricky things. My mind seems to always think about the bad stuff more than the good. It can make you feel crazy! Why is this? Why are we so quick to focus on everything negative?

Simply put, our brain defaults to the path of least resistance. It is easier for our brains to think about what's going wrong than what's going right. I am not sure why, but it seems this is always the case. Our brains always want to jump to the worst-case scenario. The truth is, we have to train our brains to look for the good things in our lives.

The Bible has a lot to say about being thankful.

Let's look at a few of those scriptures.

I will praise the Lord according to his righteousness: and will sing praise to the name of the Lord most high.

Psalm 7:17

Speaking to yourselves in psalms and hymns and spiritual songs, singing and making melody in your heart to the Lord; Giving thanks always for all things unto God and the Father in the name of our Lord Jesus Christ;

Ephesians 5:19-20

In everything give thanks: for this is the will of God in Christ Jesus concerning you.

1 Thessalonians 5:18

The Bible tells us that we should give thanks in everything we do. Why is this important? Practicing thankfulness takes our mind off all of the bad parts and focuses it back on the good. Being thankful is a deliberate action we take to retrain our brains to look for the good things in our lives.

Maybe you are so down and distraught right now it seems you can't think of a single thing to be thankful for. Start with something simple. God, I thank you that I am alive and breathing. God, I am thankful that I had food to eat today. God, I am thankful that I have clothes to wear. It might start off hard, but you will find that the more you thank God for things in your life, the more you will have to be thankful for.

Here are a few things I thank God for each day.

- God, I thank You for my health. Thank you that I have strength in my body to walk, talk and praise Your name.

- God, I thank You for a good job.

- God, I thank You that my children are healthy.

- God, I thank You that I have a place to live and food to eat.

- God, I thank You for my pets.

- God, I thank You for my church.

- God, most of all, I thank You for your salvation which is given to me free and clear!

If you truly want to change the way you think, you have to pursue a spirit of thankfulness each day. I want to challenge you to do this. Every morning, tell God 5 things you are thankful for—just five things. It can be anything you want to say—just choose five. At first, it may be hard to think of five things, especially if you are going through tough times, but I think you will find it gets easier every day. Suddenly, you will be walking through your day and see a sunset and say, "God, thank you for the beauty you have put in this world." Maybe someone will give you a helping hand, and you will say, "God, thank you so much for my friend." When you start looking for things to be thankful for, you tend to find them!

Why is thankfulness important?

What are two things in your life you can be thankful for today?

What is one thing from this chapter you can apply to your life right now?

Notes

Forbearing one another, and forgiving one another, if any man have a quarrel against any: even as Christ forgave you, so also do ye

Colossians 3:13

Chapter 11

I'm Not Sorry!

I once knew a woman who was notorious for holding grudges. If you ever crossed her path and did something she didn't like, she would remember it—forever! All these grudges caused her to become bitter. All that bitterness caused her to become a miserable person. Unforgiveness can ruin your life and make you miserable!

Has someone in your life hurt you? I know I have been hurt many times. Whenever someone hurts you, you have two choices. You can keep your anger, bitterness, and unforgiveness inside, or you can choose to let go and move on. Holding on to the unforgiveness in your heart does nothing to the person you are angry with, but it does hurt you.

Now, I need to clarify what it means to forgive and let go. If someone robs my house, I can forgive them, but that does not mean I will allow them back in my house. I am not going to invite them to dinner.

I am going to stay away from them because I know

they can hurt me. When you forgive someone, it

doesn't mean you open yourself up to be hurt again.

It just means you have decided not to dwell on what

they did and allow it to make you miserable.

Maybe you have a child or a close friend who has

offended you. If at all possible, try and mend the

relationship and move past it. You don't want to lose

a relationship over one thing someone said when

they were angry. During these times, we need to

remember that we also make mistakes and need

forgiveness from time to time.

I knew one man who struggled with unforgiveness

and bitterness so much he refused to speak to a

family member for six years because they

accidentally spelled his name wrong! Sometimes we

get angry over things that just don't matter. If today

were your last day on earth, how important would

your co-worker's snide comment be? Realizing we

are not promised tomorrow helps keep our minds

right and makes us more apt to forgive others.

What does the Bible have to say about

unforgiveness? Let's look at a few verses.

*And when ye stand praying, forgive, if ye have ought
against any: that your Father also which is in heaven
may forgive you your trespasses.*

Mark 11:25

*And be ye kind one to another, tenderhearted,
forgiving one another, even as God for Christ's sake
hath forgiven you.*

Ephesians 4:32

*Forbearing one another, and forgiving one another, if
any man have a quarrel against any: even as Christ
forgave you, so also do ye*

Colossians 3:13

*Judge not, and ye shall not be judged: condemn not,
and ye shall not be condemned: forgive, and ye shall
be forgiven:*

Luke 6:37

Since God has forgiven us so many times, how can we hold grudges and unforgiveness against others? Even more, how can we expect God to forgive us when we can't forgive others? Remember, I am not saying to allow toxic people back into your life, but you only hurt yourself by holding on to bitterness and unforgiveness.

Maybe you don't know how to let go and forgive. Realize that sometimes it is a process. It may not happen overnight, but there are a few things that can help you let go of the unforgiveness and bitterness in your life.

First of all, try to focus on the present instead of the past. It is easy to get caught up in thinking about what was done to you in the past and stop living in the present. Today, try to live your day to the fullest and do your best not to think about the past.

Whenever a thought about the past pops up, you need to focus on something happening today.

Some hurts don't heal overnight. With those types of wounds, we need the help of the Holy Spirit to let go. Sometimes you have to get up every day and ask God to bring you one step closer to forgiveness. One day, you will look back and see how far you've come. Just take it one day at a time and keep your faith in God.

Remember, forgiveness does not mean forgetting. We have all heard that phrase many times—forgive and forget. Sometimes, however, that is the total opposite of what you should do. If someone abused you, you can let go of that hurt, but that does not mean you should allow that person back in your life! You can forgive and still protect yourself from further harm.

Bitterness and unforgiveness can cause you to become miserable. When you choose to hold a grudge, you are hurting no one but yourself. When you make a conscious decision to let go, you will live a happier life, full of peace!

Why is it important to forgive?

____

____

____

____

____

Is there someone in your life that you hold a grudge against? What can you do to move past that unforgiveness?

____

____

____

____

____

What is one thing from this chapter you can apply to your life right now?

____

____

____

____

____

Notes

Forbearing one another, and forgiving one another, if any man have a quarrel against any: even as Christ forgave you, so also do ye

Colossians 3:13

Chapter 12
Spiritual Oppression

Throughout this book, we have talked about many of the different causes of depression. Depression can be caused by circumstances, chemical imbalances, toxic people, guilt, unforgiveness, and so much more. There is, however, another cause of depression that is much more sinister, and that is demonic oppression.

When my two boys were just toddlers, I experienced this type of demonic oppression. It felt like a heavy, gray cloud was pushing down on me. It felt almost like a tangible darkness had descended on my home. The day that oppression left, it felt like somebody had lifted a thousand-pound weight off my shoulders. I felt like I could breathe for the first time in months. If you are dealing with depression that almost seems like a tangible darkness, you may be dealing with demonic oppression.

Some people get confused when I talk about demonic oppression. They think I am talking about demonic possession, like when Jesus cast the demons out of the man in the Bible. This, however, is something completely different. If you are a child of God, you cannot be possessed by a devil. Why? Your life belongs to God. If Jesus lives inside of you, there is no room for the devil.

Demonic oppression is a specific, targeted attack on the atmosphere surrounding you and your home. It can feel like an intense heaviness in the air around you. This type of depression cannot be addressed by natural means and requires a spiritual remedy.

The Bible talks a lot about spiritual warfare. In Ephesians chapter 6, Paul describes to us the whole armor of God and stresses the importance of being prepared for battle. Let's take a look at those verses.

*Put on the whole armor of God, that ye may be able
to stand against the wiles of the devil.*

Ephesians 6:11

This first verse simply tells us that the devil is
tricky. If you are going to stand up against him, you
need to wear the whole armor of God. You cannot
expect to defeat the enemy in your own power.

*For we wrestle not against flesh and blood, but
against principalities, against powers, against the
rulers of the darkness of this world, against spiritual
wickedness in high places.*

Ephesians 6:12

You are not fighting a physical battle. If you were
marching in a war, we would know exactly who the
enemy is, but the battle we are fighting is spiritual.
There is warfare going on in the heavens. That is
where the real battle takes place. This type of battle
cannot be fought through conventional means. It is a
spiritual battle, and it requires a spiritual solution.

Wherefore take unto you the whole armor of God, that ye may be able to withstand in the evil day, and having done all, to stand.

Ephesians 6:13

Here, Paul tells us there is a specific armor we can put on to help us stand against the enemy when he brings on these attacks. My favorite part of this verse is when he says, "And having done all, to stand." So many times, when we are going through a battle, it takes everything just to stay upright. It is a good feeling when you can look back over a battle in your life and say, "I'm still standing!"

Stand therefore, having your loins girt about with truth, and having on the breastplate of righteousness;

Ephesians 6:14

When we are fighting a demonic oppression, the first thing we need is the Word of God. The Word of God is truth! The enemy will spend a lot of time trying to fill your mind with lies. He will try and tell you things contrary to the Word of God. We need to be able to fight these demonic onslaughts with the word of God.

Jesus used the Word when He was tempted in the wilderness by the devil. Whenever the enemy would come at Him, He would throw the truth back. The enemy can't stand in the presence of God's truth!

When the enemy says you are a loser, you remind him I am fearfully and wonderfully made. When the enemy says your going down, you remind him I am more than a conqueror through Christ Jesus. Whatever the enemy can throw at you, God has given you a scripture for it.

The enemy will also attack you with shame and condemnation. He will tell you you're not good enough and you have failed too many times. That is

why we must wear that breastplate of righteousness.
What is this? When we accept Jesus as our Savior,
we are covered by His blood. From that time on,
when God sees us, He doesn't see our
righteousness but the righteousness of Christ. The
Word says our righteousness is as filthy rags. We
will never be good enough in ourselves. Jesus
already paid the price for our salvation, so we don't
have to live in shame and condemnation anymore.
When the enemy tries to remind you of your past,
point to Jesus Christ, your future!

*And your feet shod with the preparation of the gospel
of peace;*

Ephesians 6:15

In this verse, Paul is reminding us not to forget
our shoes! Shoes? Yes, shoes! Imagine you were
in a battle with all your armor on but forgot your
shoes. One simple piece of debris in the field could

injure you and stop you from fighting. With our shoes

on, we can walk through the battlefield without fear

and keep our concentration on the real battle at

hand.

What is the Gospel of Peace? It is simply the

good news that Jesus died and rose again on the

third day and has freely given us salvation. When we

are walking in that truth, we don't have to live in fear.

When my mother was battling cancer, she wrote

this in her journal:

I'm a winner if I'm healed

I'm a winner if I die and receive a crown of life!

She understood that as long as she believed in

Christ, she didn't have to fear death or anything else

man could do to her. Your salvation was bought with

the precious blood of Christ, and no devil in hell can

take that away from you. That realization can give

you absolute peace of mind! We can walk in peace

because we know where we are going!

Above all, taking the shield of faith, wherewith ye
shall be able to quench all the fiery darts of the
wicked.

Ephesians 6:16

Faith is all about believing the promises of God

are true for your life. Even though we might not see

the fulfillment of God's promises to us, Faith reminds

us that God's word is always true! Even if we can't

see it now, He is working in the background for our

good. When the enemy attacks you, telling you all

his lies, you need to remind him of what God has

said. God cannot lie. His word will stand forever.

We can have faith that His promises are true for our

life!

And take the helmet of salvation,

Ephesians 6:17a

There was a girl I was good friends with growing up. She would always say, "I need the helmet of salvation because it protects my mind from the enemy. When he comes against me, I remind him of the work Jesus did on the cross."

When we accept Jesus as our Savior, His blood covers our sins. When God looks at us, He sees the blood. When the enemy looks at us, he sees the blood applied to our life. We are bought with a price, and the enemy can never take that away from us.

My mother came from a generation where her entire life centered around the Lord. She used to tell me, "If you feel like you are facing a demonic attack, begin to plead the blood of Jesus. Sing songs about the blood of Jesus. The devil starts running when you start talking about the blood!" Why does the devil run when you talk about the blood? It is through the blood we have salvation. It is through the blood he lost his hold on this world. It is through the blood we have won! There is power, power in the blood!

And the sword of the Spirit, which is the word of God:

Ephesians 6:17b

We have talked about this before, but I can't stress enough how important it is to speak the word to the enemy when he attacks you. When the devil tempted Jesus in the garden, He spoke the word back to him in every instance. The word is truth, and the enemy hates the truth. When you speak the truth of the word of God, you are releasing your faith into the atmosphere. You are giving God a chance to work in your situation. So when the enemy attacks you, speak the word!

Ephesians 6:18

This is the most crucial part of fighting a spiritual battle—prayer! The Bible says that prayer can move mountains. The sad thing is, when you are depressed, you don't always feel like praying. Sometimes it's the hardest thing you can do. Even though it is hard, it is your greatest weapon against the enemy. You must learn to push through and spend time talking to God.

Someone once told me, "I just don't know how to pray." You can talk to God just like you talk to your friends. Many times I am driving to work, and I just begin talking to the Lord. I thank Him for all He's done for me, then I tell Him how I've been feeling and ask Him to help me. The Bible says He hears the cry of those who are afflicted. He will hear you if you cry out to Him!

The Holy Spirit will help you when you pray. Jesus said the Holy Spirit is our comforter. Paul even said that when we are too weak to pray, the Holy Spirit intercedes for us even through our cries and groans. Can you imagine that? The Holy Spirit is interceding on your behalf! There were times I didn't feel like praying, but once I started, the Holy Spirit entered my prayers, and it became so easy!

There is also a type of demonic oppression that doesn't let go so easily. The disciples were trying to cast out a devil once, and they could not. Jesus let them know that this type of assault does not leave but by prayer and fasting. Sometimes you have to get alone with God and just cry out to him. Sometimes you have to push back a few plates so you can empty yourself of everything but God.

If you have prayed and fasted but still feel oppressed, find some anointed brothers and sisters to help you pray. The Bible says where two or three agree on anything in Jesus' name—He would do it. There is power in numbers. Put the enemy to flight by having your friends agree with you for your miracle.

There were many times we would have small prayer meetings in our home. We would just begin to pray and let the Lord lead and direct us. We saw so many miracles come out of those prayer meetings! Why? There is power when people come together and pray! When you begin to agree together and cry out to God, you will see those strongholds broken! There is power in prayer!

When there is no natural cause for your depression, you could be facing a demonic oppression. To face this kind of assault, you have to stop looking at the natural and look at spiritual things instead. You need to arm yourself with the Word of God and have faith that His words are always true and faithful. You need to have peace in knowing God has saved you and will not leave you alone. God hears you when you pray! Cry out to Him, and He will hear you and answer you in your time of need. Remember, you are not alone. Many people, including myself, have faced demonic oppression during our lives. Let me assure you of this one thing—God will not leave you there. He will always make a way of escape for you. Keep holding on to his hand and trust that He will bring you through!

What is a demonic oppression?

What are two ways you can battle a demonic oppression?

What is one thing from this chapter you can apply to your life right now?

Notes

For I reckon that the sufferings of this present time are not worthy to be compared with the glory which shall be revealed in us.

Romans 8:18

Chapter 13
He's Taking Us Somewhere!

We talked in an earlier chapter about how

sometimes depression is caused by our

circumstances. We all go through tough times, and

often that can lead to feelings of anxiety and stress.

Did you know that God sometimes uses the tough

times in our lives to bring us someplace better?

Let's look at the story of Joseph. He had it all.

He had a rich father, and he was the favorite. It

looked like everything was going his way, until one

day, his brothers got jealous and sold him to some

slave traders going to Egypt.

You might think that is where Joseph's story ends,

but actually, this is where it begins. He was a slave

in the house of one of the commanders of Egypt, but

the Bible says, "God was with Joseph." In the middle

of his slavery, God was still with Joseph and blessed

him. Did you know God could bless you right in the

middle of your mess? God began to bless Joseph, and pretty soon, he was running the whole house.

Then, something terrible happened. Does it sometimes feel like you are just dodging one problem after another? You see, someone lied on Joseph and got him thrown into jail. The Bible tells us that even in prison, "God was with Joseph." God blessed Joseph even in the jail cell! He made him head of the prison. Even if you are in a terrible place, God can bless you in the middle of your mess.

If you know the story of Joseph, you know he eventually ended up in the palace, in charge of all Egypt under Pharoah. God used the bad circumstances in his life to take him to the place he was destined to be.

Sometimes, it seems like everything in your life is falling apart. There are times when this is just God trying to get you to your destiny. Even in the middle of those times of pain, He is still with you and can bless you.

I remember a situation that happened with my sister. My sister and her husband were very active in the church they grew up in, and he had a great job that he loved. Out of nowhere, everything began crashing down around them. People came up against them in the church. Her husband lost his job—a job where he had previously won awards for his excellent performance. It looked like everything was against them.

What they couldn't see was that God had to stir things up to get them where they needed to go. They are now the Pastors of a mission church in Georgia, and my sister has an amazing job. They are reaching out to multitudes they never thought possible! None of it would have ever happened if they had not gone through those dark days. God had something better for them. They couldn't see it at the time, but looking back, they see God's hand in everything they went through.

When we are in the middle of a battle, we can't always see God's hand. We don't always know where he is taking us. Romans 8:28 tells us that all things work together for our good if we love God. He can turn our messes into blessings if we just hold on.

You may be going through the toughest battle of your life. You may not see a way out. God is still with you. He will bring you through. You may not understand the reason now, but He has a plan. He loves you and wants you to prosper. Just hold on to God and believe that He is going to work it out for your good!

Why did Joseph have to become a slave and go to prison?

____

____

____

____

____

____

Can you look back over your life and see a situation where God took something bad and turned it for your good?

____

____

____

____

____

What is one thing from this chapter you can apply to your life right now?

____

____

____

____

____

____

____

Notes

Be strong and of a good courage, fear not, nor be afraid of them: for the LORD thy God, He it is that doth go with thee; he will not fail thee, nor forsake thee.

Deuteronomy 31:6

Chapter 14
You Are Not Alone!

What was my goal in writing this book? I was so tired of the stigma Christians put on themselves when it comes to depression. For some reason, people think that if you are depressed, you are somehow not right with God, or you are weak. We have learned, however, that even the prophets of God in the Bible got depressed. Even King David, the apple of God's eye, got depressed. Christians get depressed. Yes, I said it. Christians get depressed. Weak or strong, it doesn't matter. Christians get depressed.

That does not mean we are without hope. Oh no! Our hope is in Christ, and even if we struggle in this world, we have something better waiting for us when we get to Heaven. We have hope in Jesus! You may be struggling right now, and may not see a way out. I want to tell you today—there is hope! Things may look bleak today, but there is hope! Things might feel rotten today, but there is hope! Don't give up!

You are not alone. There are multitudes of people facing the same struggles you are. Don't isolate yourself, but surround yourself with people who will build you up and encourage you.

Don't be afraid to ask for help. We all need help sometimes, and that is ok. If you broke your leg, you wouldn't stay home and say, "I can't go to the doctor because they might think I'm weak." No! You go to the doctor and get the help you need. It is no different when you are depressed. See that doctor, counselor, or other professional. Get the help that you need. You are not weak. You are just using the common sense the Lord gave you. When you need assistance, get it!

Stop feeling guilty about being depressed. I don't feel guilty if I get the flu. I get some medicine, take care of myself, and get better. You should not feel guilty because you are depressed. You should get the help you need to get better and take care of yourself.

If more Christians were open and honest about depression, I think we would see fewer and fewer news articles about Christians taking their own lives. It is ok to admit you are struggling. We all struggle. Let's ditch the stigma of depression and start being honest about what really goes on behind closed doors.

Christians get depressed. Pastors get depressed. Praise Team leaders get depressed. Everyone, at some point, goes through tough times. If someone tells you they never struggle, then they are lying! We all face hardships in life, and if we can be honest and open about it, we would reach more people for Christ than ever before. Why? People don't want to see perfection in the church. They want to see people who have been through some things, so they know they have hope in life too!

You are not alone. You may feel all alone and like you can't handle another day, but I urge you to reach out to someone for support today. You don't have to walk this path alone! Find a local church that will encourage you and build you up. Start seeking God and praying every day, even when you don't feel like it. Don't be afraid to see a professional if you need help. That's why they're there! Just know, you are not alone!

Maybe you do not currently have a relationship with God. You may not have the peace that comes with knowing you will live eternally with Christ in Heaven. If this is the case, I urge you to surrender your life to Him today. This world is tough enough to face. You don't want to have to face it without God!

If you have not accepted Jesus as your Savior, let me walk you through the steps today.

For all have sinned, and come short of the glory of God.

Romans 3:23

The first thing we must do is recognize that we are all sinners. We have all messed up sometime in our lives. We are all guilty.

For the wages of sin is death; but the gift of God is eternal life through Jesus Christ our Lord

Romans 6:23

We deserved death. We are guilty.

But God demonstrates His own love toward us, in that while we were still sinners, Christ died for us

Romans 5:8

We deserved death, but Christ died for us. He paid

the price for our sins, so we don't have to take that

punishment ourselves.

*That if you confess with your mouth Jesus as Lord,
and believe in your heart that God raised Him from
the dead, you will be saved*

Romans 10:9

Because Jesus paid the price for us, all we have

to do is believe in Him, trusting that His death is the

payment for our sins, and we can be saved!

Salvation is available to anyone who calls out to God.

*There is therefore now no condemnation to them
which are in Christ Jesus, who walk not after the
flesh, but after the Spirit.*

Romans 8:1

If you have accepted Christ as your Savior, He

will forgive your sins. You no longer have to live in

the guilt of your past. Jesus paid the price for your

sins, and you can live in His freedom today!

Notes

Notes

Notes

Notes

Notes

Notes

Notes

Notes

Notes

Notes

Notes

Notes

Notes